ST. A[illegible]S SHRIVENHAM

The Wisdom of Saint Benedict

BENEDICTVS

The Wisdom of Saint Benedict

Compiled and introduced by
Esther de Waal

Published by
Lion Publishing plc
Sandy Lane West, Oxford, England
www.lion-publishing.co.uk
ISBN 0 7459 4216 4

First edition 1999
10 9 8 7 6 5 4 3 2 1 0

Picture acknowledgments

1: St Benedict with a Book, Sacro Speco, Subiaco/Scala, Florence; 2: St Benedict by Hans Memling, Uffizi Gallery, Florence/Scala, Florence; 24: Scenes from the Life of St Benedict: The Saint receives King Totila (detail) by Spinello Aretino, San Miniato, Florence/Scala, Florence; 32: Scenes from the Life of St Benedict: The Saint Shatters a Glass of Poisoned Wine with the Sign of the Cross by Bartolomeo di Giovanni, Uffizi Gallery, Florence/Scala, Florence

9: The Saint Leaves his Father's House; 17: The Saint Obtains Flour; 18: The Saint Instructs the Peasants; 21: Romanus Gives his Habit to the Saint (detail); 26–27, 43: The Saint Makes Water Flow from the Mountain (details); 29, cover: The Devil Breaks the Bell (detail); 35: The Saint becomes Abbot, all from Scenes from the Life of St Benedict by Sodoma, Monte Oliveto Maggiore/Scala, Florence

All artwork by Vanessa Card

A catalogue record for this book is available from the British Library

Typeset in 12.5/13 Venetian 301
Printed and bound in Singapore

Contents

Introduction

St Benedict was born around the year 480 in Nursia in Italy, and while he was studying at Rome felt a call to leave the university and instead to live a life of solitary prayer in a cave at Subiaco, 'holding himself still before the gaze of God,' in the words of St Gregory the Great. This laid the foundation for what was to follow: he became the founding father of a small community of monks living at Monte Cassino in the Apennine mountains outside Rome. Here he wrote his Rule, a practical handbook or guide helping them to impose on their lives a rhythm which recognized the role of body, mind and spirit, praying, studying and working – that balanced life of the Benedictine tradition.

This short text, no more than 9,000 words, although it was written over 1,500 years ago and intended for men in rural Italy, has become one of the great spiritual classics. Increasing numbers of lay people from all denominations are turning to it for practical help and inspiration in today's world. The Rule comes from hard-won experience, written by a man with a good grasp of the human psyche and who himself knew the demands of living with oneself, the equally demanding task of living with others, of handling the tools of daily life, and of trying to make prayer the one essential reality.

The fact that St Benedict was never a priest is something that we should not overlook, for we often tend to forget that monasticism was essentially a lay movement. The abbot was *abba*, father, the exemplar of Christ, to this extended family of brothers, who like any of us knew about the continual round of preparing food, looking after the sick, entertaining visitors, maintaining buildings and property. St Benedict wanted to impose on this busy life such a structure and order that prayer became its centre. There was no separation of prayer and life, of praying and living.

The first word of the Rule is Listen: listen to the Word. 'Today if you hear my voice harden not your hearts.' This is an invitation to become open, transparent to the Gospel, to the command of love, to the person of Christ.

St Benedict is concerned not so much with achievement as with the disposition of the heart. Of course we will fail, but he gives us the tools; for the Benedictine vows are not poverty, chastity and obedience, but vows that can be applied in any Christian's life. *Conversatio morum*, or continual conversion, is to be open to the new, to journey, to follow the call of Christ wherever it may lead. But then, since the Rule, like the Gospel, is a way of paradox, he tells us to stand, to stay firm, for stability means that we do not try to run away; not in any geographical sense but in the more profound sense of being rooted or earthed in our interior selves, standing still before God. And the vow of obedience (from the Latin *ob-audiens*: to listen intently) means that we try at each step of the way, and each moment of decision, to hear and to discern what God wills for us, so that we listen, hear and respond by saying Yes.

The three together point us towards the paschal mystery, to the figure of Christ, who was obedient to the will of his father, who was steadfast and persevering in the demands of love, and who journeyed in the way of the cross. This way, for Christ as for all who follow him, is the way of new life, new birth, resurrection.

ESTHER DE WAAL

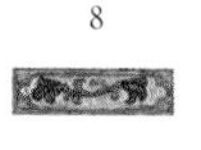

THE JOURNEY

I

The Call

However late, then, it may seem, let us rouse ourselves from lethargy. That is what scripture urges on us when it says: the time has come for us to rouse ourselves from sleep.[a] Let us open our eyes to the light that shows us the way to God. Let our ears be alert to the stirring call of his voice crying to us every day: today, if you should hear his voice, do not harden your hearts.[b] And again: let anyone with ears to hear listen to what the Spirit says to the churches.[c] And this is what the Spirit says: Come my children, hear me, and I shall teach you the fear of the Lord.[d] Run, while you have the light of life, before the darkness of death overtakes you.[e]

Rule, Prologue 8–13

2

THE WRONG SORT OF JOURNEYING

Those called gyrovagues are another kind of monk. They spend their whole life going round one province after another enjoying the hospitality for three or four days at a time of any sort of monastic cell or community. They are always on the move; they never settle to put down the roots of stability; it is their own wills that they serve as they seek the satisfaction of their own gross appetites.

Rule, 1:10–12

3

The Path of Life

Who is there with a love of true life and a longing for days of real fulfilment?[a] If you should hear that call and answer: 'I', this is the answer you will receive from God: If you wish to have that true life that lasts for ever, then keep your tongue from evil; let your lips speak no deceit; turn away from wrongdoing; seek out peace and pursue it.[b] If you do that, he says, I shall look on you with such love and my ears will be so alert to your prayer that, before you so much as call on me, I shall say to you: here I am.[c] What gentler encouragement could we have, my dear brothers and sisters, than that word from the Lord calling us to himself in such a way! We can see with what loving concern the Lord points out to us the path of life.

Rule, Prologue 15–21

4

Ascending through Descent

If we are eager to be raised to that heavenly height, to which we can climb only through humility during our present life, then let us make for ourselves a ladder like the one which Jacob saw in his dream.[a] On that ladder angels of God were shown to him going up and down in a constant exchange between heaven and earth. It is just such an exchange that we need to establish in our own lives, but with this difference for us: our proud attempts at upward climbing will really bring us down, whereas to step downwards in humility is the way to lift our spirit up towards God.

This ladder, then, will symbolize for each of us our life in this world during which we aspire to be lifted up to heaven by the Lord, if only we can learn humility in our hearts. We can imagine that he has placed the steps of the ladder, held in place by the sides which signify our living body and soul, to invite us to climb on them.

Paradoxically, to climb upwards will take us down to earth but stepping down will lift us towards heaven. The steps themselves, then, mark the decisions we are called to make in the exercise of humility and self-discipline.

Rule, 7:5–9

5

The Way of Salvation

If we want to avoid the pain of self-destruction in hell and come to eternal life, then, while we still have the time in this mortal life and the opportunity to fulfil what God asks of us through a life guided by his light, we must hurry forward and act in a way that will bring us blessings in eternal life…

In the guidance we lay down to achieve this we hope to impose nothing harsh or burdensome. If, however, you find in it anything which seems rather strict, but which is demanded reasonably for the correction of vice or the preservation of love, do not let that frighten you into fleeing from the way of salvation; it is a way which is bound to seem narrow to start with. But, as we progress in this monastic way of life and in faith, our hearts will warm to this vision and with eager love and delight that defies expression we shall go forward on the way of God's commandments.

Rule, Prologue 42–49

6

The Final Question

Are you hastening towards your heavenly home?

Rule, 73:8

STABILITY

7

Building on Rock

The Lord himself in the gospel teaches us the same when he says: I shall liken anyone who hears my words and carries them out in deed to one who is wise enough to build on a rock; then the floods came and the winds blew and struck that house, but it did not fall because it was built on a rock.[a]

Rule, Prologue 33–35

8

The Dwelling Place

We should make our own the psalmist's question: Lord, who will dwell in your kingdom or who will find rest on your holy mountain?[a] In reply we may hear from the same psalmist the Lord's answer to show us the way that leads to his kingdom: anyone who leads a life without guile, who does what is right, who speaks truth from the heart, on whose tongue there is no deceit, who never harms a neighbour nor believes evil reports about another,[b] who at once rejects outright from the heart the devil's temptations to sin, destroying them utterly at the first onset by casting them before Christ himself.[c] Such a follower of Christ lives in reverence of him and does not take the credit for a good life but, believing that all the good we do comes from the Lord, gives him the credit and thanksgiving for what his gift brings about in our hearts.

Rule, Prologue 23–29

9

Standing Firm

If novices after two months show promise of remaining faithful in stability, they should have the whole of this Rule read to them and then be faced with this challenge at the end: that is the law under which you ask to serve; if you can be faithful to it, enter; if you cannot, then freely depart. Those who still remain firm in their intention should be led back to the novitiate so that their patience may be further tested. After another six months the Rule should again be read to them so as to remove all doubt about what they propose to undertake. If they still remain firm, then after four more months the same Rule should again be read to them... They must by now be fully aware that from that day forward there can be no question of their leaving the monastery nor of shaking off the yoke of the Rule, which in all that time of careful deliberation they were quite free to turn away from or to accept as their way of life.

Rule, 58:9–16

Obedience

10

The Importance of Obedience

It is not easy to accept and persevere in obedience but it is the way to return to Christ, when you have strayed through the laxity and carelessness of disobedience. My words are addressed to you especially, whoever you may be, whatever your circumstances, who turn from the pursuit of your own self-will and ask to enlist under Christ, who is Lord of all, by following him through taking to yourself that strong and blessed armour of obedience which he made his own on coming into our world.

Rule, Prologue 2–3

11

The Narrow Way

Those who are possessed by a real desire to find their way to eternal life don't hesitate to choose the narrow way to which our Lord referred when he said: Narrow is the way that leads to life.[a] They live not to serve their own will nor to give way to their own desires and pleasures… No one can doubt that they have as their model that saying of the Lord: I came not to do my own will but the will of him who sent me.[b]

Rule, 5:10–13

12

The Obedient Will

The first step on the way to humility is to obey an order without delaying for a moment. That is a response which comes easily to those who hold nothing dearer than Christ himself... Of such servants of his the Lord says that they obeyed him as soon as they heard him.[a]

Rule, 5:1–4

13

GOD'S HELP

If instructions are given to anyone in the community which seem too burdensome or even impossible, then the right thing is to accept the order in a spirit of uncomplaining obedience. However, if the burden of this task appears to be completely beyond the strength of the monk or nun to whom it has been assigned, then there should be no question of a rebellious or proud rejection, but it would be quite right to choose a good opportunity and point out gently to the superior the reasons for thinking that the task is really impossible. If the superior after listening to this submission still insists on the original command, then the junior must accept that it is the right thing and with loving confidence in the help of God obey.

Rule, 68

14

Imitating Christ

The second step of humility is not to love having our own way nor to delight in our own desires. Instead we should take as our model for imitation the Lord himself when he says: I have come not to indulge my own desires but to do the will of him who sent me.[a]

Rule, 7:31–32

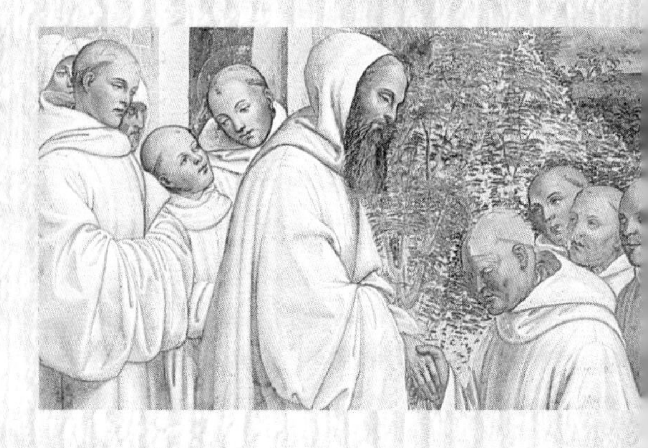

15

Perseverance until Death

We shall never think of deserting God's guidance; we shall persevere in fidelity to his teaching in the monastery until death so that through our patience we may be granted some part in Christ's own passion and thus in the end receive a share in his kingdom. Amen.

Rule, Prologue 50

16

Patient Endurance

The fourth step of humility is to go even further than this by readily accepting in patient and silent endurance, without thought of giving up or avoiding the issue, any hard and demanding things that may come our way in the course of that obedience, even if they include harsh impositions which are unjust. We are encouraged to such patience by the words of scripture: whoever perseveres to the very end will be saved.[a] And again there is the saying of the psalm: be steadfast in your heart and trust in the Lord.[b] Then again there is that verse from another psalm: it is for you we face death all the day long and are counted as sheep for the slaughter.[c]

Those who follow in that way have a sure hope of reward from God and they are joyful with St Paul's words on their lips: in all these things we are more than conquerors through him who loved us.[d]

Rule, 7:35–39

The Heart

17

The Listening Heart

Listen, child of God, to the guidance of your teacher. Attend to the message you hear and make sure that it pierces to your heart, so that you may accept with willing freedom and fulfil by the way you live the directions that come from your loving Father.

Rule, Prologue 1

18

Searching the Heart

The first step of humility is to cherish at all times the sense of awe with which we should turn to God. It should drive forgetfulness away; it should keep our minds alive to all God's commandments; it should make us reflect in our hearts again and again that those who despise God and reject his love prepare for themselves that irreversible spiritual death which is meant by hell, just as life in eternity is prepared for those who fear God.

One who follows that way finds protection at all times from sin and vice of thought, of tongue, of hand, of foot, of self-will and of disordered sensual desire, so as to lead a life that is completely open before the scrutiny of God and of his angels who watch over us from hour to hour. This is made clear by the psalmist who shows that God is always present to our very thoughts when he says: God searches the hearts and thoughts of men and women,[a] and again: the Lord knows the thoughts of all,[b] and: from afar you know my thoughts,[c] and again: the thoughts of men and women shall give you praise.[d]

Rule, 7:10–17

19

A Pure Heart

If in ordinary life we have a favour to ask of someone who has power and authority, we naturally approach that person with due deference and respect. When we come, then, with our requests in prayer before the Lord, who is God of all creation, is it not all the more important that we should approach him in a spirit of real humility and a devotion that is open to him alone and free from distracting thoughts?

Rule, 20:1–3

20

THE SIMPLICITY OF PRAYER

The oratory must be simply a place of prayer, as the name itself implies, and it must not be used for any other activities at all nor as a place for storage of any kind. At the completion of the work of God all must depart in absolute silence which will maintain a spirit of reverence towards the Lord so that anyone wishing to pray alone in private may not be prevented by the irreverent behaviour of another. Then also anyone who at some other time wants to pray privately may very simply go into the oratory and pray secretly, not in a loud voice but with tears of devotion that come from the heart.

Rule, 52:1–4

Love

21

The Love of Christ

Any monk or nun who has climbed all these steps of humility will come quickly to that love of God which in its fullness casts out all fear. Carried forward by that love, such a one will begin to observe without effort as though they were natural all those precepts which in earlier days were kept at least partly through fear. A new motive will have taken over, not fear of hell but the love of Christ. Good habit and delight in virtue will carry us along. This happy state the Lord will bring about through the Holy Spirit in his servant whom he has cleansed of vice and sin and taught to be a true and faithful worker in the Kingdom.

Rule, 7:67–70

22

Loving God, Loving Others

The first of all things to aim at is to love the Lord God with your whole heart and soul and strength and then to love your neighbour as much as you do yourself. The other commandments flow from these two…

The way to become holy is faithfully to fulfil God's commandments every day by loving chastity, by hating no one, by avoiding envy and hostile rivalry, by not becoming full of self but showing due respect for our elders and love for those who are younger, by praying in the love of Christ for those who are hostile to us, by seeking reconciliation and peace before the sun goes down whenever we have a quarrel with another,[a] and finally by never despairing of the mercy of God.

Rule, 4:1–2, 63–74

23

Equal Love for All

The abbot or abbess should not select for special treatment any individual in the monastery. They should not love one more than another... One who is freeborn should not, for that reason, be advanced before one coming to monastic life from a condition of slavery, unless there is some other good reason for it. If such a reason is seen by the abbot or abbess to be justified they can decide on a change for any member of the community. Otherwise all must keep their proper place in the community order, because whether slave or free we are all one in Christ and we owe an equal service in the army of one Lord, who shows no special favour to one rather than another.[a]

Rule, 2:16–20

24

Young and Old

Juniors in the community should show due respect for their seniors, and seniors should love and care for their juniors. When they address each other it should not be simply by name, but senior monks call their juniors 'brother' and the juniors address their seniors as 'nonnus' or 'reverend father'. The abbot is understood to hold the place of Christ in the monastery and for this reason is called 'lord' or 'abbot', not because he demands it for himself but out of reverence and love of Christ.

When members of a monastic community meet each other, the junior asks a blessing of the senior. As a senior passes by, the junior rises and yields a place for the senior to sit down and will never sit without the senior's permission. In that way they will conform to scripture which says: they should try to be the first to show respect for each other.

Rule, 63:10–17

25

THE GOOD SHEPHERD

The abbot or abbess... should show equal love to all and apply the same standards of discipline to all according to what they deserve.

They should make their own the different ways of teaching which the Apostle Paul recommended to Timothy when he told him to make use of criticism, of entreaty and of rebuke.[a] Thus in adapting to changing circumstances they should use now the encouragement of a loving parent and now the threats of a harsh disciplinarian. This means that they should criticize more sternly those who are undisciplined and unruly; they should entreat those who are obedient, docile and patient so as to encourage their progress; but they should rebuke and punish those who take a feckless attitude or show contempt for what they are taught...

They should reflect on what a difficult and demanding task they have accepted, namely that of guiding souls and serving the needs of so many different characters; gentle encouragement will be needed for one, strong rebukes for another, rational persuasion for another, according to the character and intelligence of each. It is the task of the superiors to adapt with sympathetic understanding to the needs of each so that they may not only avoid any loss but even have the joy of increasing the number of good sheep in the flock committed to them...

However many the souls for whom they are responsible all superiors may be sure that they will be called to account before the Lord for each one of them and after that for their own souls as well. Frequent reverent reflection on that future reckoning before the Good Shepherd who has committed his sheep to them will, through their concern for others, inspire them to greater care of their own souls. By encouraging through their faithful ministry better standards for those in their care, they will develop higher ideals in their own lives as well.

Rule, 2:22–25, 30–32, 37–40

26

The Spirit of Love

It is easy to recognize the bitter spirit of wickedness which creates a barrier to God's grace and opens the way to the evil of hell. But equally there is a good spirit which frees us from evil ways and brings us closer to God and eternal life. It is this latter spirit that all who follow the monastic way of life should strive to cultivate, spurred on by fervent love. By following this path they try to be first to show respect to one another with the greatest patience in tolerating weaknesses of body or character. They should even be ready to outdo each other in mutual obedience so that no one in the monastery aims at personal advantage but is rather concerned for the good of others.[a] Thus the pure love of one another as of one family should be their ideal.

Rule, 72:1–8

PRAYER

27

Praying with Others

God is present everywhere – present to the good and to the evil as well, so that nothing anyone does escapes his notice; that is the firm conviction of our faith. Let us be very sure, however, without a moment's doubt that his presence to us is never so strong as while we are celebrating the work of God in the oratory. And so we should always recall at such times the words of the psalm: serve the Lord with awe and reverence,[a] and: sing the Lord's praises with skill and relish,[b] and: I shall sing your praise in the presence of the angels.[c] All of us, then, should reflect seriously on how to appear before the majesty of God in the presence of his angels. That will lead us to make sure that, when we sing in choir, there is complete harmony between the thoughts in our mind and the meaning of the words we sing.

Rule, 19

28

Praying Alone

We really must be quite clear that our prayer will be heard, not because of the eloquence and length of all we have to say, but because of the heartfelt repentance and openness of our hearts to the Lord whom we approach. Our prayer should, therefore, be free from all other preoccupations and it should normally be short, although we may well on occasions be inspired to stay longer in prayer through the gift of God's grace working within us.

Rule, 20:1–4

29

Praying for Forgiveness

It is important that the celebration of Lauds and Vespers* should never be concluded without the recitation by the superior of the whole of the Lord's prayer so that all may hear and attend to it. This is because of the harm that is often done in a community by the thorns of conflict which can arise. Bound by the very words of that prayer 'forgive us as we also forgive' they will be cleansed from the stain of such evil.

Rule, 13:12–13

* *the monastic offices of morning and evening prayer*

30

Praise

The words of the psalm are: I have uttered your praises seven times during the day.[a] … About the night Vigil that same psalm says: In the middle of the night I arose to praise you.[b] And so at these times let us offer praise to our Creator.

Rule, 16:1, 4–5

Text acknowledgments

The extracts in this book are taken from *Saint Benedict's Rule: A new translation for today*, Patrick Barry OSB (former Abbot of Ampleforth), Ampleforth Press, 1997, distributed Gracewing Ltd, with the exception of extract 6, which is taken from *The Rule of St Benedict*, edited Timothy Fry OSB, Liturgical Press, Collegeville, Minnesota, 1980.

In his text Patrick Barry has not included numbered verses, but these have been given beneath the extracts so that readers who wish will be able to find them in any of the numerous alternative translations and editions available.

Bible references are as follows:

Extract 1 a: Romans 13:11; b: Psalm 94(95):8; c: Revelation 2:7; d: Psalm 33(34):12; e: John 12:35. Extract 3 a: Psalm 33(34):13; b: Psalm 33(34):14–15; c: Isaiah 58:9. Extract 4 a: Genesis 28:12. Extract 7 a: Matthew 7:24–25. Extract 8 a: Psalm 14(15):1; b: Psalm 14(15):2–3; c: Psalm 14(15):4 and cf Psalm 136(137):9. Extract 11 a: Matthew 7:14; b: John 6:38. Extract 12 a: Psalm 17(18):44. Extract 14 a: John 6:38. Extract 16 a: Matthew 10:22; b: Psalm 26(27):14; c: Psalm 43(44):22; Romans 8:36; d: Romans 8:37. Extract 18 a: Psalm 7:9; b: Psalm 93(94):11; c: Psalm 138(139):2; d: Psalm 75(76):10. Extract 22 a: Matthew 5:44–45; Ephesians 4:26. Extract 23 a: cf Romans 2:11. Extract 25 a: cf 2 Timothy 4:2. Extract 26 a: Romans 12:10. Extract 27 a: Psalm 2:11; b: Psalm 46(47):7; c: Psalm 137(138):1. Extract 30 a: Psalm 118(119):164; b: Psalm 118(119):62.

Further books by Esther de Waal on Benedictine spirituality:

Seeking God: The way of St Benedict, new edition in preparation
A Life-Giving Way: A commentary on the Rule of St Benedict, Geoffrey Chapman, 1995
Living with Contradiction: An introduction to Benedictine Spirituality, Canterbury Press, 1989, 1997

Books on Cistercian spirituality:

The Way of Simplicity: The Cistercian tradition, Darton, Longman & Todd, 1998
A Seven-Day Journey with Thomas Merton: Making a private retreat, Eagle, Guildford, 1992
(Intended to be used by people who do not have the time or money to go away on retreat.)